WHIRLING ROUND THE SUN

To Mort Lichter & Gordon Rogoff
"And say my glory was I had such friends"
from yours, however new,
    Suzanne Noguere   July 2013

WHIRLING ROUND THE SUN

Poems by

Suzanne Noguere

Midmarch Arts Press, New York

Library of Congress Catalog Card Number 96-076462
ISBN 1-877675-22-9

Printed in the United States of America

Published in 1996 by
Midmarch Arts Press
300 Riverside Drive
New York, New York 10025

for Henry Grinberg

Like to the lark

CONTENTS

I

EAR TRAINING FOR POETS

As the owl in darkness zeroes in
on the world's small sounds, so must you. But which?
The deepest comes from any quiet room
where you can lie down undisturbed. So wait
and listen. Do waves wash a distant shore
over and over? What ocean? What land? Too low
for anyone but you, your heart beats and
repeats its proof that you are musical.

Wait until you hear this; then go on.
And if you can, leave your room at the start
of spring and linger by the maples as
their leaves push out fully formed but folded:
accordion-pleated along the veins.
There is a song here for the catching when
the leaflets spread—a murmur but half heard,
a melody where April and maple meld.

Then on your city streets, be keen, for words
are always floating through the air like seeds.
Listen as two friends part and one calls back,
"I meant to mention...": how the sounds seem
to grow by mitosis, taking their function
from position as at first in embryos
the cells do, this one becoming heart, that brain.
Compare this with the past. Have these principles
always been at play, as when Lesbia's sparrow

qui nunc it per iter tenebricosum
is pulled along the line's dark corridor
and swallowed up? So may you be
swallowed up in tenderness for your tongue.

(There is no need for you to listen for love
since your ear naturally magnifies
its slightest sound: as just one molecule
of scent diffused in air will draw the moth
from miles away to meet a mate, so just
three syllables can draw you half way
around the world—who knows for what?)

Now this is the hard part: to hear your life
slipping away. Listen at odd moments
while waiting on line, catching a bus,
washing your clothes, or paying bills, and try
to hear it go as softly as a needle
moving through cloth. Now you are closing in
on silence, whose beats you must at last learn
to count evenly as in music or
as when love bids goodbye for good.

THE RECITATION

When the monosyllables of Wang Bo
fell from your lips that night with their strange weight,
not strange to you, as we sat by the fountain
turned pool in a city fearful of drought,

the rain began so lightly that I thought
it was an ethereal dancer who
pranced before us in a pensive mood,
setting a toe down here, now there, in slow

motion so that the pool sparkled distinctly.
Then I glanced sidelong at you, at both
your eyes reflecting the lights of the world,
your mind reflecting on its dark, your teeth

each varied in the ivory curve that shaped
every sound on a new principle.
Then the words and the drops glistened. I saw
the seconds of my life made visible.

PERVIGILIUM VENERIS

Like the white whale, born black, myself grows brighter
year by year until at last my prime,
if it comes, should dazzle as a paradigm
of transformation; or as if the night were
about to leave a pupal cave and light were
one instant signal to forget the time
of the shamed slow-motion caterpillar climb,
I wait for wings that are more hale though slighter.

Winter-born by chance, my youth was frozen.
When will my sun shine? When will Apollo
look back for me and let me know how long
before that spring is coming that I've chosen?
When is the year I shall be as the swallow
that I may sing my one specific song?

THE SCRIBES

THESCRIBESPACKEDCAPITALSACROSSTHEPAGE
as if they were still chiseling stone until
at last in minuscules they fixed a wedge
of space between the words and a hush fell
upon the page as if light filtered through
trees to a forest floor. It is the space
inside the vessel, said Lao-tzu,
that is its usefulness. It is the space
inside the u that gives it life. And where
the leaflets of the white ash meet the stalk,
not sessile but set a space apart, the air
moves in between them in the give and take
of interpenetration, as nearing
the end, the poem itself comes to a clearing.

LUCRETIUS

Lucretius, not for you the myth
of the phoenix rising from the flames
or any other, but if
there is a grain of truth in what
they say about your madness, might
it be that in the calm nights while
you watched the heavens revolve
and fixed the words like constellations
on the scroll, once from
the midnight oil the midnight owl
rose in a wreath of fire to
inspirit you with its own wild
wisdom and the thrust of wings?

ATOMOLOGIES

The sky, the sea, the earth, the creatures, crops,
and all the worlds beyond our own arose
by chance as atoms bonded in the void.
So I read you, Lucretius, and suppose
that you read Epicurus with this same
zeal to confirm his thought. For where you say
the atoms have a finite set of shapes
but infinite combinations the way
letters interchanged make different words,
I want to amplify like you and cite
new proof: how your own letters rearranged
have made this other tongue in which I write
as atoms in outer space make other worlds.
And in this one how slight the shift between
live and love, between hate and heat, and how
much clearer what you guessed at can be seen,
that we are each the me of memory.
And if the wish that your epic cure us of
the fear of death and of the gods did not
still bind us to you, then this would above
all else: the discipline of the line
that rolls the universe up in one verse,
then spreads it out from speck to cloud to show
your heart a rearrangement of the earth.
How nature governs and what wisdom is—
by steps you lead us where the mind still longs
to go, to linger on those lucid heights
where you, Lucretius, create us your songs.

ROBERT JOHNSON

When Mr. Johnson has the blues you'd think
that glass would crack, floors jolt, and the needle coax
from the spinning disk his yet unsettled ghost

as genies have been rubbed from lamps—if not
his ghost, at least that genius of a muse
who made the blues apocalyptic news.

Is it she, heard falsetto through his voice,
who is the ultimate ventriloquist,
or is it he whose prodding makes the gist

come from the dummy sitting on his knees?
It talks, tells, urges, cries, chimes, and rings
and yet it is nothing but wood and strings.

Bent over his aggrieved guitar and bent
on being, all the same he doesn't shrink
to come so early to the brink

of death; for every Southern song has taught
the heart that always goes for broke can't last
longer than to write its fast epitaph.

And it is useless, sitting here, to wish
for once to see the smile or hear the laugh
of the dead man pleading from my phonograph.

BARNEY BIGARD

Solo or in the ride out gliding and
soaring through three and a half octaves like
the swallow-tailed kite sure in air on land

and sea and seeming half on fire in quick
drops through the cypress swamp, its white and jet
feathers fanned like palmetto, making thick

gloom glorious, swooping as if to whet
the heart with startling grace, he makes the air
move, peerless and clear, in the clarinet.

In chalumeau it comes out, *la chaleur*
of New Orleans, in upper range the reck-
less runs he mastered in Chicago where,

when King Oliver asked him to go back
to the hard instrument the Tios taught,
he stood amidst the live and water oak

in spirit, bent his own will like a note,
and worked until all tones below the staff
were the dark blue of the great river's throat.

There are days when the mind amazes itself
with phrases and keen, melancholy breaks
that state the facts exactly, as if

the mind itself were heated like the wax
of an unpressed record, ready for the die
casting of indelible phrases as

his fingers spring from the fast keys, then fly
back into the black wood with a Creole cry.

THE SECRET

Nathaniel, born Hathorne, you who set
the scarlet letter A on Hester's bosom
as the world's avenging epithet
to scorch the roots where it had found the blossom,
what secret was there in your own heart when
you slipped the W into your name?
Some Wilderness you would not yield, a green
reserve where in their privacy thoughts came?
Or was it Wonder always at your core?
Or Witch or Woman, Will, or Word to mark
the curse upon your name in Salem lore
and at the same time sever from that dark
inheritance? Or deeper than a double
meaning, was there a double you akin
to the small thorned tree whose branches are brambles
where a songbird is safe? Was there a twin
heart in the heartwood forming slowly, tough
as oak, that paced your twelve-year solitude?
Was hardiness in poor soil a proof
of possibility? Or thorns amid
the whitest flowers in spring the truth in view?
The berries?—scarlet in winter! Now, small tree,
if there be any empathy in you,
take to yourself that last emphatic E.

ON THE EXISTENCE OF FICTIONAL CHARACTERS

If Hamlet ever lived in Elsinore,
no grave gives proof. No epitaph on stone
or reliquary brings the visitor
to pay homage to one so near the throne
as, even in the world backdoor
at St. Helena, changing guards had shown
honor to the ex-man, ex-emperor.

A difference of flesh, of dust. How does
it matter that a Paris tomb contains
these relics from Marengo: some favored clothes
dressed on what little corporeal remains
of *Le Petit Caporal*? Suppose
the body had been burned, the face and brains
ceremoniously scattered where the seawind blows.

A person perished and a ghost survived
to haunt the mind as Hamlet does with his
distress. Who's there? we ask. Who's there who lived?
Napoleon advances from the world that was
into the world where life must be believed—
for see how since your father's death he is
the mythical being your mother loved.

THE PAPER SPEAKS

Pen and paper. You make it sound like bread
and butter or, as I'd say, sun and rain.
I seem to have survived the saw
and caustic bath since once again I'm thin,
flat, wide—a scrap of what I was but still
alive, albino now and bare. I feel
you scratch the words out a dozen times,
trying every which way to find their valence.
Don't think I don't understand! You want
the words to bond. You want a charge to jump
from one word to the next and link them up
in a chain you can balance on your tongue
and find by its very nature sweet.
Don't struggle so. Put down your pen and I'll
absorb your energy out of thin air
and fix it in a form to nourish life.
Now let me do it as I did when leaf.

MULBERRY

I have been mulling over your life,
white mulberry, so woven into mine
by the young Chinese empress Xi Ling Shi,
who saw a silkworm devour your green
serrated leaves, then spin a thread around
itself, a ghost in gossamer twine.

And I have been wondering what effect
your leaf-shapes had upon the Japanese
as they tied the silk up in such bold
diagonal designs to dip in dyes,
taking perhaps from your one lobe or three
or six the element of surprise.

And I have been musing on how for years
the American colonists sought rewards
in vain by planting you in hope of silk.
But now while your wild berries bring you birds
I'll feast on leaves and try to spin and hide
myself inside a filament of words.

SEWING WITH MY GREAT-AUNT

Today you bend over organdy,
working a row of small red squares
as in your youth old men bent over earth,
coaxing wheat and corn from the Basque soil.
You fold the cloth, then slowly roll the edges
until rose petals bloom in your hands,
vivified by the stitch that shirrs them softly
the way the skin is shirred around your eyes.

We overlap the petals; roses thrive
under the lamplight in your wintry room.
Next you teach me the genesis of frogs:
we turn the tubing, and fresh cloth emerges
out of itself like a snake sloughing its skin.
You whorl it tightly till it seems to be
how your great spirit must exist in you
compactly, coiled like a spring.

"Do you remember the trip to Lourdes?" I ask
as your hand digs deep in a doll-sized pocket.
"*Bien sur*, but the Virgin was sleeping that day,"
you say, armored in humor and charm as then,
a child praying in vain to grow, bound home
not with the mystery of miracle
but the mystery of fate, sitting beside
the mother to whom you were a cross and curse.

Crooked like a mitered edge, your index finger
at rest stays poised above an unseen needle.
Now you show me buttons made from thread
and dresses that unfold as if corollas
with minute parts inside. You ground me in
techniques as secret as nature's, my fingers
sure when yours are, atremble when yours falter
those sharp days when you feel more and more mortal.

EXTREMITIES

The doctor calls it *ulnar drift,* the way
your fingers now curve outward on both hands,
the bones driven like snow. So this is winter,
when fingers no longer work, not from cold
but age. It is no use for me to thread
the needle you cannot hold, or hope to see
cloth other than this blanket in your hands,
where veins rise like tree roots from eroded soil.

Day after day you lie on your back in bed
as if testing the feel of eternity.
Two years not touching earth, your toes
have curled under like a bird's around a branch
and won't let go of something invisible.
And I have read how already the bones
of your legs, as still as in a grave,
must be turning to dust from disuse.

My bones make the same blood as yours; and in
their hollows the same echoes tell me how
that lowering day's at hand when I must
see six feet between us, if I can stand it.

ONE MORNING

as I coiled my hair, a strand
caught on a fingernail,
the two dead parts of my body locked
like thread at the top of a spool—

I tugged the hair a little the way
I saw my mother free the thread
so many times when I was a child,
then bend her head

eye to eye with the needle
and start to hem the dotted swiss
or corduroy I'd run my hand across
like a picket fence.

Her stitches skimmed the glow
of a rose print or a royal blue
equally the aqua of a pool:
the dresses I outgrew

the way I slipped from her embrace.
I pulled the snagged hair taut
and felt the prick of memory
with its quick root.

MY GRANDMOTHER NELLIE BRAUN

Age took the old ache of that girlhood fall
from the barge roof onto the wooden deck
and humped her back so that she stood as tall
as her last grandchild at ten; her neck-
length hair, cut blunt and snooded, became as coarse as
sailmakers' thread. Bright eyes belied all flaws:
"I don't drink, gamble, or play the horses,"
she said, explaining the long distance calls.

Florida was farthest; was that daughter dearest?
Who could go to snowed-in, strange Vermont?
Four paths from Brooklyn left her still the nearest
source of kind worth, of simple sweetness, font;
and where she sat was center on each inner map,
with her hands folded in her quiet lap.

THE CHILD

In the prologue the mother had no lines.
Directions said that she should sit upstage
but left the acting to her own designs—
she could knit baby sweaters to engage
the audience or stroke her cauled confines.
Her action as analyzed on the page
was to sit, to let her belly's signs
loom like a ghost or shadow: to presage.

Yet when the curtain rose the scene was bland:
some players, chairs, a table, dishes, mop,
all paraphernalia the playwright planned
to use as the heavy and dull-skinned strop
on which to sharpen well his reprimand,
understating how the players would swap,
clothe, feed, caress, and pass from hand to hand
the child who seemed like a perfect prop.

Years passed on the stage like a ball of yarn
that fell and in a second would unroll
the toil of hours and of being born;
yet the child stayed fixed in her child's role
and having met with neither joy nor scorn
had only herself in her dying soul
to be the agent for herself and warn
of the passivity that could not console.

Move and be seen by a million eyes?
Shout with a voice that had never known rage?
Dare to approach and touch a lover's thighs?
Dare to be judged by a moving gauge?
The fear overgrown in the end denies
all contentment with its cramping cage.
Actress or heroine, without disguise
she spoke her lines and walked across the stage.

THE LOOM

It stood there in the middle of the room,
a plain wood frame, simple and sturdy yet
so often untouched: the loom for a poem.
But now she sat in front of it and stretched
the rhyme scheme down its length as a warp thread
the lines as weft would interlace. She kept
a rhythm going as she wove that made
the warp seem harp strings that her fingers swept.
And sometimes as she beat the weft together
she thought she heard the ocean pound the land,
and then the weft seemed not just thread but rather
rows of ripples imprinted on the sand.
And as the cloth revealed its pattern, once
she thought she heard it murmur in her own voice.

III

SOMA

This body deemed machine—not daemon flesh
that makes itself from a given seed and springs
up in a reptile's egg with the bones of a fish,
from fins makes fingers and four telic limbs—
propels each cell into the fetal mesh
to feed and be fed by the heart, brain, and lungs.
But on the off chance that this might not be,
try Ockham's razor on that trinity.

My heart keeps up its obbligato to
my every thought, intrudes its presence as
I fall asleep feeling its to-and-fro,
so that it seems a mackerel swims in place
beneath my ribs, delaying death just so
long as it keeps on moving. Yet this ace
half pound of muscle never falters, fit
to function: matter with a mother wit.

My brain's empowered by that primal pluck
but almost could believe itself the critter
superior to all, for watch it shuck
off body with an avid thrust the better
to be the avatar proclaimed a book—
as if the body of one's work were fitter
with its glittering spine shining on the shelf
to house that essence of oneself, one's elf.

And all the while still the brain's high notion
of its own inspiration follows from
the sole exemplar of the lungs in motion.
Not housed; inherent; everything I am—
each grief, belief, and elemental passion—
starts and snaps with this living frame.
Account me compost when my lungs are through
and the true salt water of my blood turns blue.

Then colonies of me in their remote
substrata, cells that rallied with each omen,
will perish one by one and bring about
the dissolution of my soul, my soma.
Lying without a pulse or breath or thought,
my body steels itself in that long moment
before it festers, as it cools to ice.
It will not witness Halley's comet twice.

DILLINGER

Wouldn't they know it was Red anyway
by those two fingers sliced off his right hand
like so much meat when he was still a kid?
The man he'd trusted, but the corpse would talk
if the law found it: fingertips like hot bills—
on file, numbered, unmistakable.
Hamilton's body lay there to be buried.
He poured lye on the lifeless face and hands.

It wasn't fun any more to see
his own face clear as in a mirror on
the front page with that fat reward: five grand
in five states. He would give that much to have
a new face, to wake up with memory
intact and see a self that didn't shout
from a scar near the lip, on the wrist,
from the chin dimple DILLINGER.

It was his own face gone askew he saw
when the ether wore off. O god! No good!
Now all he hoped was that the acid would
eat through his fingers to the flesh and stop
the cells of his skin in their dogged march
upward through five layers, more persistent
than his worst pursuers, always in
the strict formation of his fingerprints.

Borne to the morgue less than two months later,
he might still have escaped the law but for
the whorls emerging in familiar arcs:
between scars, the skin's indomitable remnants.

HANDS

I

My hands are
each asymmetrical with five
fingers fixed at different heights like the
heads in a family
snapshot—

a shape
curious, if not queer
with the thumb off on its tangent, the whole
explicable only by the
laws of chance

II

They mirror
each other, looking like equals
as they clasp or clap or cup water but
nothing could be more a
fiction

for as
my right hand wields the pen
and rushes to complete a thought, my left
hand smoothes the paper, helping out
like a child

III

When I sit
they are always in front of me
moving about, so you'd think I'd see them
more than anything else
on earth

In truth
I don't notice, as now
what I see are the words I am writing,
paper and pen recede, my hands
disappear

IV

If I were
blind, my hands might learn to read, my
fingers touching the white page lightly as
if each word were a snow
crystal

If I
were deaf, my hands might learn
to speak, my fingers flinging themselves out
with the intensity of ten
born dancers

V

On my five
fingers I count my five senses,
then count them again on my other hand,
reciting each like a
blessing

I say
touch and my hands reach from
bark to bud to leaf and make it seem no
accident that their name contains
the word *and*

VI

Sometimes my
left hand curves and holds the arc just
like the great wave off Kanagawa in
the thirty-six views of
Fuji

Sometimes
my right hand opens up
in the time-lapse sequence of a flower
blooming all at once atop its
single stem

VII

On the back
of my hands the tendons extend
to finger bones segmented in columns
the way the Chinese paint
bamboo

Over
them the veins spread in blue
branchings as if a great river coming
down through my arm had at last reached
the delta

VIII

My plump palm
shows nothing but surface, its skin
cross-hatched and thick but nonetheless a text
a palmist might read for
meaning:

the life
line circling my thumb, the
grooves for heart and head, and below them the
death line I drew on my wrists at
seventeen

IX

It fell to
my hands to answer once and for
all the who? who? who? like an animal
cry sounding through my brain
for years

Armed in
mortal combat they went
for the pulse point, wounding each other while
the pulse kept on trying to make
itself heard

X

Steady as
waves breaking, the pulse repeated
itself until my hands heard it, a speech
not human, pre-human,
in me

saying
beneath the who, the what,
a creature equal to the tree against
my back, whole, here, and my life was
in my hands

WHIRLING ROUND THE SUN

Sometimes it seems almost beyond belief
to be here whirling round the sun: this view
of buildings taller than trees, trees, and the blue
sky unmoved like a truth graphed on the chief
coordinates of my window frame. Yet leaf
by leaf turning gives my slow mind a clue
to earth's revolution and with such hue
sometimes it seems almost beyond belief
to see. As a bus speeds me through the park
past maple, sourgum, and sweetgum's clearer
color, so fast along my nerves the sparks
fly to my brain with their electric sign
for scarlet, then make my mind a mirror
of amber; and the effort is not mine.

MY WORLD

looks fine in blueprint; it is a small green-
house of my own through which all day the sun
shines evenly. To give more heat, pipes run
the building's length and breadth, so that between
the sun and pipes it takes no great routine
to run this house; it runs itself; and one
can spend all day inside yet not be done
with raising buried seeds to a bloom's sheen.

I try to make each flower strong enough
to live its season, if only to be
dried in a dusty album. As for the dangers
to my glass house, I cannot weed, breed, or snuff
them out; and, nights, reflected in its panes I see
a face always stranger than any stranger's.

THE MEANS

Sensuous to the nth degree, this end
result of ordered atoms (organs and
electric pulses through live tissue) pleads
for fabric in its fingers, silk and tweeds
to feel; as eyes always have their pick
of toucan colors to look at and like.
Won by words, then ears heed tunes as tongues
make them; as a tongue tastes the simmered tangs
of garden soup and that good smell is grasped.
How the body holds fast to pleasure, hasped
by penchant, as if its deep molecular
linked nitrogen with carbon and water were
meant for that only, part and whole, as if
the body at its pith were not itself
another piece of native earth, a plot
where love the last laurel will root or rot.

IV

THE LETTERS

Now the pale paper shows, the darker too,
but once they came like precious presents, wrapped.
Love was the spell; spelled out, still veiled, too new
to know for a sole maiden mind not apt
to deem words solid but must doubt and dove-
tail tender greetings with the taint of fears—
till idioms first ionized for love
were neutralized into the salt of tears.

They are tied up like old newspapers not
to be reread: half of a packet, half
the words where all would not uncover what
went wrong, the hesitation and rebuff,
the mute misgivings leading to the waste
of disbelief that made that first love chaste.

THE RENDEZVOUS

A corner table and the room so dark
that soon the other tables disappear
and I'm alone with you, not face to face
but closer, side by side, to be that near.
I turn to trace the gray wave of your hair
and at this angle your profile is
as pale and chiseled as the crescent moon.
Then you turn to me full face, luminous,
whether with your own or my reflected light
it is too late to tell. At last we lower
our eyes; then all the phases of your face
compress months of waiting into one hour.

A KISS

What is a kiss? Not the kind that blends
into the next, moving from yes to depth
in a slow legato that forks the legs,
but the kind we have, the one that ends
our visits like a punctuation point.

It is a quest: for as our lips collide
in that billionth of a second buss
like particles accelerated in a beam,
we seek the irreducible first form of love.
I track it across your face: *now*, then *was*.

BOTANICAL SKETCH OF YOU

Saguaro I'd say if I had to
compare you with a plant:
you are that tall and straight and apt to
stand apart in silhouette.

And prickly! I've seen your cactus
spines in action as a string
of words almost tactile
in the way they sting.

To brave them is to find a home
in you, my own deep wish,
as the woodpecker carves a room
in saguaro flesh.

And you have known how to store up love
in memory's net
and been able to stay alive
through years of drought,

not withering but with the strength
to splurge and draw
on those reserves of succulence
you use to flower now.

THE CASUAL LOVERS

Self-centered in the first assault
upon each other, strangers part
without regret. Yet by the eighth
time they meet and overwhelm
each other's senses wholly, they
linger hand in hand and halt
mid-sentence in a vow of faith,
presaging each may have to pay
for ravishment as in the realm
of Hammurabi, heart for heart.

THE BOTTLE

I found it at the fair: Mrs. A's
Honey of Horehound, just the bottle with
those words embossed, for what had been inside
had long since been taken by mouth.

No matter; it's not a cold that ails me but
this fever that you gave me with a potent
cure in mind. I read your smile: Mr. J's
Honey of Hormones, guaranteed. Just open.

WE WHO IN

love's circus do love's fireball feat: eat
the witching flames; and lit by our own spotlight eyes vie
who is the better bareback rider; leonine then try
to tame the other into a sweet defeat—
our hearts have stilts: our very legs and feet—
and it's a clowns' finale when we lie and ply
our juggling trade, forgotten faces wry,
all to turn the trick and so increase this heat.

By day no one would guess our nightly act,
that we could be such stars in center ring,
and we are almost used to balancing
high-wire over your normal world and mine.
Whatever words the future may exact,
may *vale* never touch this valentine.

CONTINENTS

How much of me is land, a mass, mere crust
moved by subterranean forces that
reveal themselves but rarely? Must
I shake with tremors to penetrate
my depths? See lava to know that molten magma
flows endlessly beneath my surface? Cite
and hold in my two hands the hard cold fragment
to call it by name, basalt or kimberlite?
Stolid in our calmest year, I wondered
at a slight shifting, nothing much, when it
swelled and a force tore through my core and sundered
even us. So when South America split
off Africa's new jagged edge: one hundred
million years do not erode the fit.

THE MUSIC BOX

Like studs once stamped on a revolving disk,
inside me your words catch on a star-wheel
and surely pluck my nerves tuned like the steel
teeth of an antique music box. I risk
the tune again. How could I think to ask
for music I had never heard? Or feel
less than rare myself when your appeal
makes me its resonator, gear, and cask?

You tell me of the arctic night's pale blue,
of Africa, far Asia, and the sight
of nations rising and of soldiers thronging.
And yet you travel that far inward too,
can calculate depth and distinguish height.
I know you can tell me the length of longing.

YOU SAY

You say my lower
lips glow like the rose rim of
    the pink-mouthed murex

    Ah, my hermit crab,
I say they call you home where
    you enter and fit

EYES AND FLOWERS

All day my irises make minute adjustments
as light streams through the window and dims by
turns, striking the irises you brought me.
If my spirit had the speed of eyes,
I might have matched your shifts from glow to glare.
But now the flowers raise their blue hue and cry
in a pitch beyond my hearing, and their stems
are cut more cleanly with a knife than I've
been cut with words. It seems another life
when the love atoms scattered throughout me
would rise to the surface at your touch
like plankton rising through the sea at dusk.

THE DISTANCE OF STARS

The stars stared back at me one country night
as if to say, "We are the world's memory
made visible. These rays left us light-years
ago." So past was present in my eyes.

And in my heart you were like the stars,
still shining from the past. Such ancient ties
we touch again; in more than reverie
your warmth to me now is my future light.

VIEWS OF ROME

On Trajan's Column in this view of Rome
St. Peter stands in the emperor's place,
as odd at first glance as a bird atop
an elephant's back in that African
province Rome ruled, for from the column base
a spiral band ascends, carved with scenes
unknown to Peter: how the troops set out
for Dacia, built roads and forts, and fought
the rebel tribe in battles so fierce that as
the spiral spins its story face after face
gets left behind—until Trajan, somber
as the thundercloud of Jove, more just,
grants Decebalus good terms of peace, only
to be betrayed and fight the same war again.

Four centuries ago with Trajan's statue
like the lands along the Danube long
since lost, the Romans raised St. Peter; and
on the column of Marcus Aurelius,
depicting battles he would rather not
have fought, they raised St. Paul, so restoring
the columns' function and honoring them all.

In this view of our romance, a spiral
winds through you such as winds through me, not just
the double helix in each cell that marks
us with a history older than Rome,

but a spiral of the spirit carved
with the faces of those whom the twists
of fate have left behind: some whose kindness
was an unbroken stream, whose wisdom
was rosehips growing inside the rose, whose art
was a redwood always reaching higher
and evergreen; and some for whom to be
alive meant to be at war, whom we had
not wished for foes; and there the faces of those
who reappear as steady as the moon.

So as today we raise each other in
the sight of all and pledge support throughout
ages to come, joining spirit with law,
condensing our history in this choice,
and putting the past to new purpose, may
we look as odd as saints so that our view
be so vast, the arms outstretched, the feet so fixed.

WITH THEIR HEADS

jutting like gargoyles from the trees, the snakes
lie still as statues where the monkeys caper
until for one too young there is no escape or
even tearing those mosaic coils; it takes
the cawing the macaw in gaudy splendor makes
from its towering tree to warn the tapir
that the scent it has not sensed, that weight and shape are
the jaguar. Terror-struck the tapir stakes
its life on racing for the river, where
the scarlet ibis with its eyes this dark—
two specks of coal to fuel a feathered flare—
full now and fleetingly released from slaughter,
unbends its wings and neck from that double arc,
becoming air as the fish fits into water.

Turbo marmoratus LINNÉ

Born to the castle life, inheritor
of pearl, this prized green turbo on my table,
now cleaned of those soft parts from which the label
Mollusca was derived, seems to gleam the more
for being brought to land from the depths offshore.
Only now, pumice stone in hand, am I able
to see the shimmering pink and green unstable
sheen hidden by the outer shell before.

Past royal cup of Scandinavian kings,
this marine marvel of a spiral is just
the thing so ravishing it might elude
all laws. But no: alive, its maker clings
to habit; shrinks within its turret; must
stay still all day, then crawl all night for food.

SANDPIPERS

Sandpipers mirrored
on wet sand, you in my mind,
the seagull's shadow

ATLANTIC MACKEREL

The back of the mackerel gleams
green-blue to steel-blue with stripes
running down to the silver belly,
all iridescent and not scaly
to eye or hand. I have a theory
or two about that beauty.
First: that the striped pattern mimes
the waves as the fish swims.
Or else that underseas perhaps
an Oriental master dips
his brush in ink and writes a poem
on that smooth back as if it were a scroll.
And I would gladly school
with mackerel to read that poem
and fathom that open ocean home.

SELF-PORTRAIT

As I dozed in the meadow, my hair grew like grass.
By the sea my eyes were the patch of sky
that bodes a storm; my eyebrows hovered
like the tern's wings in flight.
I traveled inland and descended caves;
a coolness filled my nose and mouth and ears
as if they were another set of chambers.
In the desert my body blended with
the undulations of the dunes until
skin and sand melted into one mirage.
In the woods I was both trunk and crown.
And everywhere I went the earth was quick
to claim me with camouflage.

SKYWRITING IN JUNE

is an event, no matter if the plane
was chartered by some advertising group
to urge consumption of a drink or dupe
us otherwise; what always makes me crane
my neck is the heralded legerdemain
and acrobatics that it takes to loop
letter to letter with tail-end smoke, to swoop
on a blue spot and make the message plain.

But if the sky were my own page to fill,
I'd have it speak about the moods of clouds;
how cirrus forms high up where the wind feigns
to run ten fingers through its hair; how still
blue the sky holds its breath, a cloud, then shrouds
us in double darkness when it rains.

A ROBE

A robe blows open—
silk lining...the maple leaves
on their silver side

HORSE CHESTNUT

Horse chestnut with your name that crosses kingdoms;
your leaf: the continents just split apart;
your flowers: white towers only bees can visit;
your aura: Aurelius, majestic and good;
your wool: red homespun to warm the bud;
your leaf scars: horseshoes retired from use;
your fruit: a mace that is carried high;
your seed: the garnet that was locked away;
your crown: a nimbus never dimmed, horse chestnut!
No one denies the divine right by which
you wear and vary it: in spring the sky's
own garden, in summer an umbrella flecked
with emerald, in fall the first prophet,
in winter Shiva in his cosmic dance.

ELM

Elm: the elemental word whose root
means nothing but itself like *mother, sun,
heart, one,* the unanalyzable *lm—*
that speciated in the tongues of Europe
and lodged in the colonists' minds
to cross the ocean in a boat.

Elm! They knew that leaf: unequal at
the base like the two sides of any question
and each one doubly toothed. But not wych elm
and not the English. Never had they seen
an elm as elegant as this that towered
and flared into a vase-shaped crown that seemed
to hold a flock of birds like flowers.

Kaṍkæ:? So the Iroquois
called the tree, one word for their six tongues,
one unanalyzable root that proved
the tree was central to their life. They knew
its moods. They knew its willingness in spring
to yield its outer bark to knife and wedge
as if it were a cloak too warm to wear.
They peeled the bark and left the tree to heal,
bearing the bark back sheet by sheet to sew
onto the longhouse frame. What was their League

itself but a longhouse with six fires
stretching from the Hudson to the Genesee?
And who were they to themselves but
the *Hau de no sau nee,* "People of the Long House,"
who gave thanks to the Creator, thanks to
the earth, the sun, the streams, thanks to the trees.

Red man and white, friends on a land still forest,
tangled together for one hundred years.
But who now were the English to themselves?
Loyalist or *Patriot, Tory* or *Whig*—
words seared the air like bullets
and caught the Iroquois in the cross-fire
of an ire they did not understand.
Like the mid-vein of a leaf, straight and strong,
neutral between both sides, beseeched, they said
for one year, two, "Brother, we love you both."
But as sap oozes out when a leaf is torn,
so the blood flowed from their veins too, blood
the color of skin, brother against brother,
the League split open by the hatchet of hate,
two nations to the rebels, four to the British,
red and white intermingled on both sides
and everywhere the cornfields burning and
the houses going up in flames.
                              Peace brought
white settlers streaming west until

the Iroquois were hemmed in on reservations,
and where the settlers came they cleared the land,
cleared the land and planted the elm, the vaulting elm
that made Main Street a cathedral aisle.

II

Ceratocystis ulmi: the fungus spread
by elm bark beetles as they flew from tree
to tree through Europe after World War I
with the spores stuck like pollen on their backs,
feeding and breeding in bark along a route
of devastation for ten years before
they lodged in the logs meant for veneer
and crossed the ocean in a boat.

Ceratocystis ulmi: certain death,
the causal agent of Dutch elm disease,
specks on the beetles as they breach the bark,
specks that are spores, spores that bud into more
and flow in the sap stream throughout the tree
and spread their threads along the vessel walls,
tangled and toxic, then breed into more
until at last the tree fights back to block
their way with growths jutting into the stream,
with gums clogging its own lifeline to the leaves.
Without water the leaves turn yellow, and

wilt follows. Branch by branch and year by year
the thirst worsens and still the tree stands, rooted
like a people to their ancestral land.

Elm, the American elm, the skeleton elm
standing by roadsides in the rigor of death,
surviving in pockets like the Iroquois
in a stubborn otherness not skin deep
or in the elm all told in a vase shape
but reaching deeper into every cell
to the double sum of its chromosomes,
twice that of every other elm on earth.
Now spring comes and we scout the trees for wilt.
We strip the bark to look for discolored wood.
With saws and shovels, fungicides and pheromones
we take to the field; and in the lab, creative
in crisis, we wait out new ways to breed
resistance into what will not cross, trying
by hook or crook, by wile or will,
to save something of what we mean by *native*.

AT CUMAE

O Sibyl, will you speak to us who come
in fear of being sealed alive in doom
like flies in amber? Everywhere we fell
the forests massed like armies on our soil
or rain down acid on the mountainsides,
the ravaged earth strikes back. Now drought and floods
are Scylla and Charybdis come to prey
on lands that stretch as featureless as the sea.
On one side the ground is a baked clay jar
lying in shards; on the other, where
the rains still reach, both men and earth are swept
in torrents headlong to a river crypt.
Where trees once kept the rooted earth from slides
and drank the rain and gave it back to clouds,
now creatures flee us and the birds fly off,
and we are left with just ourselves as if
to stare into five billion mirrors that
reflect a surface glare. O seer, do not
write your oracles on fallen leaves
lest a breeze scatter them throughout your caves,
but speak aloud we pray, as long ago
you told Aeneas of the golden bough
to pluck and proffer to Pluto's wife
for passage through the underworld and safe
return. To us who have brought hell to earth,
o priestess, teach a way back or forth!

From deep within the caves the answer came:

Know that Apollo crowns no one with laurel
where laurel is once cleared.

SUGAR MAPLE

Sugar Maple, sugar maker,
here the line between
winter and spring is scored
in your bark and clean
through to catch the prize:
your sap when it starts to rise.

To the Iroquois sweet water
made you chief of trees;
and I would join their rite
with incense, thanks, and pleas,
saying in honor of your stores,
"Maple, this day is yours."

But we would not ask your favor
till your fortieth year;
then if you yielded us
forty quarts of clear
sap when it all had run,
we'd boil them down to one.

I have reached that age—turned forty
in a flash it seems—
and once again my raw
and overwintered themes
surge through my nerves like sap.
Now it is time to tap.

AMONG THE MAPLES

Today as I was walking among the maples
I saw with my own eyes the red shift
astronomers find in the spectral lines
of stars. But this was not the faint starshine
caught on a photographic plate, but green
to red on my retina as the leaves turned
and flew upward in a gust of wind
like galaxies speeding out of sight.

And then the leaves fell back to earth as if
to show me how the universe might fall
back upon itself and start again
if it has matter to rein in the stars.
And if it doesn't, then the stars must fly
in one direction only like my life.

NOTES

"Ear Training for Poets"
qui nunc it... "who now goes on the dark road" (to death)
Catullus III, line 11.

"Pervigilium Veneris"
The title is taken from the early fourth-century Latin poem "The Vigil of Venus," now attributed to Tiberianus.

"Atomologies"
The word was coined by Paul Friedländer in his article "Pattern of Sound and Atomistic Theory in Lucretius," *American Journal of Philology* 62 (1941) 16–34.

"Robert Johnson"
Mississippi Delta bluesman, 1911–1938.

"Barney Bigard"
Jazz clarinetist, born in New Orleans in 1906, died in California in 1980. The Tios were Lorenzo, Sr.; his brother Luis; and Lorenzo, Jr., masters of the Creole clarinet style. Barney Bigard studied clarinet with Luis and Lorenzo, Jr. but was playing tenor saxophone when he went to Chicago in 1925. He joined the Duke Ellington Orchestra in late 1927 and stayed until 1942.

"The Secret"
Hawthorne's great-great grandfather John Hathorne (1641–1717) was a magistrate in the 1692 Salem witchcraft trials. Legend has it that one of the condemned put a curse upon him and his descendants.

After graduating from Bowdoin College in 1825, Hawthorne retreated to his family home in Salem and spent 12 years in seclusion, writing *Fanshawe* and *Twice-Told Tales*.

He himself plays with the word *hawthorn*, saying in his introduction to "Rappacini's Daughter" that the tale comes from the writings of M. de l'Aubépine, *aubépine* being French for hawthorn tree.

"Soma"
Ockham's razor, named after William of Ockham (c. 1285–1349), is the principle of economy in explanation.

In some mackerels, the opercular muscles that move the gill covers have disappeared almost completely, and the fish must swim without rest to have a flow of water over the gills.

"Dillinger"
John Dillinger's confederate John "Red" Hamilton was killed in April 1934. In June Dillinger was declared Public Enemy No. 1 for his series of bank robberies and murders in the Midwest, and in July he himself was killed at the age of 31.

"Elm"
Kaōkæ:? is the Seneca word for the American elm (*Ulmus americana* L.); see *Iroquois Medical Botany* by James W. Herrick (Syracuse University Press, 1995).

The six nations making up the Iroquois Confederacy are the Mohawks, Oneidas, Tuscaroras, Onondagas, Cayugas, and Senecas. When they were at last forced to take sides in the American Revolution, the greater part of the Mohawks, Onondagas, Cayugas, and Senecas sided with the British, their long-time allies, and the greater part of the Oneidas and Tuscaroras with the rebelling colonists. It was not the Confederacy alone that was rent asunder: within each nation and even within families, some members chose one way, some the other.

All elms worldwide have 28 chromosomes except the American elm with 56. This "chromosome barrier" has stood in the way of successfully crossbreeding the highly susceptible American elm with Asian elms resistant to Dutch elm disease. Research activity is intense and proceeding on many fronts.

"Sugar Maple"
The Iroquois hold their one-day "Thanks to the Maple" ceremony in spring when the sap begins to run. They burn tobacco as an incense offering.

ACKNOWLEDGMENTS

Grateful acknowledgment is made to the editors of the magazines in which the following poems first appeared:

Artist and Influence: "The Recitation"; "Robert Johnson"; "My Grandmother Nellie Braun"; "The Child"; "Dillinger"; "My World"; "The Letters"; "A Kiss"; "The Casual Lovers"; "Continents"; "The Distance of Stars"; "Views of Rome"; "Sandpipers"; "Skywriting in June"

The Classical Outlook: "Atomologies"

Gradiva: "Lucretius"; "Whirling Round the Sun"

Heresies: "Sewing with My Great-Aunt"; "Extremities"

Jazz: "Barney Bigard"

The Literary Review: "The Scribes"

Lullwater Review: "Soma"

Modern Haiku: "A Robe"

The Nathaniel Hawthorne Review: "The Secret"

The Nation: "The Paper Speaks"

Pivot: "Ear Training for Poets"; "Mulberry"; "One Morning"; "Botanical Sketch of You"; "The Music Box"; "Eyes and Flowers"; "Atlantic Mackerel"; "Self-Portrait"; "Among the Maples"

Poetry: "Pervigilium Veneris"; "The Means"; "With their heads"; "*Turbo marmoratus* Linné"

Sparrow: "The Loom"; "We who in"; "Horse Chestnut"

Prairie Flower Press published "Hands" as a limited edition chapbook; Aralia Press reprinted "The Scribes" as a keepsake; both under the direction of Michael Peich. "Pervigilium Veneris" was also included in *The Poetry Anthology 1912–1977*, edited by Daryl Hine and Joseph Parisi (Houghton Mifflin, 1978). "The Scribes," "The Secret," "Whirling Round the Sun," "Soma," and "Barney Bigard" were also included in *A Formal Feeling Comes: Poems in Form by Contemporary Women*, edited by Annie Finch (Story Line Press, 1994).

"Elm" received the Gertrude B. Claytor Memorial Award from the Poetry Society of America in 1989.

I would like to thank four friends for the invaluable help they gave me with this book: James V. Hatch, reader/advisor from first to last, who read the manuscript in its rawest form and gave it shape; Stuart Miller, whose close reading necessitated and inspired many a revision; Edmund Pennant, whose advice and encouragement have been a constant support and resource; and Cynthia Atkins, whose sense of the synergy between poems found possibilities I hadn't seen. I would also like to give my deep thanks to Emile Capouya and Daryl Hine for first publishing my poems over 20 years ago; to Dana Gioia for creating opportunities for me; to Martin Mitchell for bringing me into the community of poets; to Alfred Dorn for his kind support; to Janice Levit for permission to use a photograph by Herschel Levit in the artwork (lake with clouds, bottom page 44); to my brother Philip Noguere, who set me on this path; and to my publisher, Cynthia Navaretta, the beacon at its end.

My special thanks to David Wander, who brought a rich imagination, a deep sympathy, and an enormous range of skills to creating the art for this book.

David Wander is an artist who works in many media. Born in New York City, he studied painting and printmaking at Pratt Institute. A portfolio of his prints was published for the Yad Vashem Museum in Jerusalem. His paintings and sculptures are in major collections throughout the world. For this book he used pen and brush as freely as the computer to create digital collages.

Suzanne Noguere was born in Brooklyn and studied at Barnard College, graduating with honors in philosophy. Over the last 20 years her poems have appeared in many periodicals, including *The Nation, Poetry, The Literary Review, Jazz,* and *Heresies.* Her work has also been published in the anthologies *The Poetry Anthology 1912–1977* (1978) and *A Formal Feeling Comes: Poems in Form by Contemporary Women* (1994). She won the 1996 "Discovery"/ *The Nation* Prize and the 1989 Gertrude B. Claytor Memorial Award from the Poetry Society of America. The author of two children's books, she lives in New York City. This is her first collection of poems.

Cover: David Wander
Cover production: Stacey Lubin
Typesetting: Barbara Bergeron
Photograph back cover: Donna Rogers Kranich

MIDMARCH ARTS BOOKS SERIES
Documenting Women in the Arts

Gumbo Ya Ya: Anthology of Contemporary African-American Women Artists

Expanding Circles: Women, Art & Community

Camera Fiends and Kodak Girls II: 60 Selections By and About Women in Photography 1855-1965

Camera Fiends and Kodak Girls I: 50 Selections By and About Women in Photography 1840-1930

Michelangelo and Me: Six Years in My Italian Haven

The Lady Architects: Lois Lilley Howe, Eleanor Manning, and Mary Almy, 1893-1937

Modernism & Beyond: Women Artists of the Pacific Northwest

Yesterday and Tomorrow: California Women Artists

No Bluebonnets, No Yellow Roses: Texas Women in the Arts

Pilgrims and Pioneers: New England Women in the Arts

Women Artists of the World

American Women Artists: Works on Paper

other MIDMARCH ARTS BOOKS

Tarnished Silver: After the Photo Boom — Essays on Photography, 1979-1989

Beyond Walls and Wars: Art, Politics, and Multiculturalism

Mutiny and the Mainstream: Talk That Changed Art, 1975-1990

Parallels: Artists / Poets

Illuminations: Images for "Asphodel, That Greeny Flower"

Images From Dante

Voices of Women: 3 critics on 3 poets on 3 artists/heroines

Artists and Their Cats

The Little Cat Who Had No Name

When Even the Cows Were Up

Artists Colonies, Retreats & Study Centers

Whole Arts Directory

Guide to Women's Art Organizations and Directory for the Arts